100

About the Author

Timothy Bay is a freelance editor and writer. He has worked as a newspaper reporter, as an editor on a business trade paper, and as a copywriter. Most recently, he helped edit *What To Do With the Rest of Your Life*, a Catalyst Career Guide for women, published by Simon & Schuster.

How to Turn Problems Into Solutions:
Solutions:
A Manager's Guide

How to Turn Problems Into Solutions: A Manager's Guide

by Timothy Bay

A HANDS-ON MANAGEMENT GUIDE

NOT FOR RESALE

EXECUTIVE ENTERPRISES PUBLICATIONS CO., INC.
33 WEST 60TH ST., NEW YORK, N.Y. 10023

PRENTICE-HALL, INC.
ENGLEWOOD CLIFFS, New Jersey 07632

ISBN 0-917386-72-8 {EXEC. ENT.}
ISBN 0-13-435669-1 {PRENTICE-HALL}
ISBN 0-13-435651-9 {PRENTICE-HALL, PBK}
Library of Congress Catalogue No. 81-69249

INTRODUCTION TO HANDS-ON MANAGEMENT GUIDES

How to Turn Problems Into Solutions: A Manager's Guide is the fourth in a management know-how series published by Executive Enterprises Publications Co., Inc. Each book in the series digests the essence of the best, the most current, and the most practical ideas in management.

The stress of unexpected daily crises, the too often neglected long-term planning, the crush of personnel problems, the avalanche of memos, proposals, and minutes from meetings are only some of the nerve-racking pressures besieging managers today. A critical factor in these ever-mounting demands on the manager's time is the enormous amount of required reading. The material may be vital for the organization's welfare, or essential for the manager's career development, but who has the time? In one survey of 500 chief executives, 415, or 83 percent, said they lacked the time to keep up even with reading in their own field. How, then, can they find the time to read the piles of books offering the newest insights into management techniques?

This series is designed to meet that vital need for information to help managers do their best job of managing. Each book will:

- Describe a management process step by step;
- Alert managers to the most frequent and costly problems;
- Offer practical suggestions on how to solve the problems;
- Define key terms;
- Digest key theories and ideas;
- Narrate case illustrations of problems and solutions;
- List a bibliography of major publications on the subject.

Book #4 deals with problem solving and decision making, which, when effectively used, function as a springboard for resourceful and productive management. The bibliography lists the books and articles from which this digest is drawn.

Myrna Lebov
Series Editor

CONTENTS

INTRODUCTION

PROBLEM SOLVING and DECISION MAKING. It may seem at first that these are strange bedfellows—two separate and distinct responsibilities of the manager. Decision making, however, is an integral part of problem solving, and vice versa. There would be no decision to make if there were no problem to solve.

In fact, decision making is an outgrowth of problem solving, coming after the study of the problem and leading to the selection of a plan of action to eliminate or overcome that problem. But effective decision making can take the manager one step further. It can turn adversity into good fortune. It can force the manager to use the problem as a springboard for developing new and creative ways of managing while furthering the objectives of the organization.

Whether corrective or creative, group or individual, decision making is a cornerstone of management. Many management experts consider it the most important aspect of the manager's job. A leading figure in modern management theory, Herbert Simon, viewed decision making as if it were synonymous with managing. In his classic text, *The New Science of Management Decision*, Simon declared that managers should seek out decision-making opportunities—find occasions for making a decision, developing courses of action, and then choosing among those courses of action. He saw decision making as a dynamic process in which managers constantly strive to overcome obstacles placed between where they are and where they want to be. The problem then is an opportunity, and the decision a way for the manager to improve the procedures and policies of the organization.

Despite the importance of problem solving and decision making, many of us still rely on an intuitive approach, using ad hoc methods instead of systematic analysis. For years, in fact, many managers treated decision making in just that way, without any kind of formal method. This is what a reporter from *Fortune* magazine found when he interviewed top businessmen for an article on "How Businessmen Make Decisions" (*Fortune*, August 1955). The majority of the businessmen interviewed did not know, or could not verbalize precisely, how they made decisions.

Since then, however, there has been growing recognition of the need for a precise and step-by-step approach to the whole decision-making process. This recognition has kept pace with the growing complexity of decision-making theory. Mathematical models and systems analysis techniques have taken decision making into the rarified realm of complex statistical formulas and abstruse probability theories. But one doesn't have to be a mathematical wizard to make intelligent and creative decisions, as this book will show.

Problem solving and decision making should follow a logical and methodical sequence, as outlined here. This building-block approach leads to a clearer understanding of obstacles and objectives. It takes you step by step through the whole problem-solving and decision-making sequence: from identifying and then analyzing the problem, through developing and evaluating alternative solutions, to selecting an alternative that satisfies your objectives. This method is valid if the manager is to make a decision alone or, as is increasingly advocated today, in cooperation with employees at all levels of the organization—in the spirit of "consensus management" (see p. 34).

The building-block approach will help you avoid the error of decision makers who, relying on strictly intuitive approaches, fail to make effective decisions because they do not fully define their objectives or understand the range of available solutions. It will also help you avoid one of the biggest pitfalls in decision making: letting your assumptions get in the way of your judgment and objectivity.

This method will lend credibility to your eventual decision. On the one hand, it reduces the danger of making decisions distorted by prejudices, personal needs, or emotions. On the other hand, it shows others that you and your staff have thoroughly investigated, analyzed, documented, and brainstormed the decision. There is, of course, no way of making risk-free decisions, but a careful and wide-ranging analysis of the issues should lead you to more intelligent, reliable, and creative decisions.

PART 1: What's happening?

You are faced with a problem. Before jumping to conclusions, find out if what you think is happening is *really* happening. Do you understand how this problem developed? Can you separate the symptoms from the cause? And what are you going to do about it?

1. CONSULT GOALS

Problem: Is This Up to Standard?

"I don't think the sales staff's performance has been really that bad," Frank Harris noted. "You have to remember that business has been bad throughout the industry . . . and that there have been major changes in our sales staff recently." A sales director for a menswear company, Harris was discussing a recent sales report with company President Donald Wollheim.

"You're suggesting that we don't look upon it as a problem, then?" Wollheim replied. "I think you're wrong. Looking over our goals for the year, I see we're in serious trouble in this area. We'll have to do something if we expect to meet those goals," Wollheim continued, "or even just to continue near an acceptable standard of performance."

*   *   *   *   *

Step 1: Consult Goals

Your goals should be your Early Warning System alerting you that something is wrong. According to the theory of management by exception, operational goals should provide the manager with an indicator of how things are going, a standard against which to compare what *is* happening with what *should* be happening. These standards are based on the averages of past performance along with projections of future performance. With a good knowledge of performance standards, the manager can easily identify *deviations*. Problems, according to management experts, can be defined as deviations from expected performance, schedules, or procedures.

The cornerstone of the operation is goal setting, says David A. Emery in *The Compleat Manager*, and "it is clearly the most important responsibility of a manager." The whole purpose of goal setting, he continues, is to "establish a sound set of criteria to guide managerial decision-making."

You should work closely with your staff (and you or they should work with lower-level employees) to develop goals along with acceptable standards of performance to achieve them. That way you and your staff will be able to recognize immediately when a problem occurs. At the same time, people sharing common goals, especially those they helped to develop, will feel greater commitment to what they are doing.

Management experts suggest that you have in writing the key points discussed during these goal-setting sessions. Whenever possible, use intervening objectives—a weekly or daily standard of performance—to direct you toward achieving those goals.

How to Set Goals

1. *Discuss options for long- and short-range goals with your subordinates, your peers, and your superiors.* Involve rank-and-file workers in the process. Department and division goals should mesh with overall organization goals. Questions to keep in mind include: What would you like to see initiated or achieved by the end of the quarter? by the end of the year? How can performance be upgraded? How can morale be improved? What can you do to get an edge on the competition? How can you improve the company's image with the public, and within the organization? Compare past performance with what you would like to see happening in the future.

If you believe you might have overlooked an important goal, Emery suggests a practical tool: a checklist that would include such categories as manpower, money, machines, material, and time. Then, from the perspective of each of these categories, look for possible improvements in operations under your control.

2. *Specify the time, place, and quantity of each of the chosen goals.* Exactly when should the goal or project be completed? Where is the completed work needed? What quantity should you aim for? If you want to step up production in a certain area, determine what your target level is, and when it should be achieved. Again, your staff will help you zero in on these issues.

3. *Set broad priorities.* Differentiate between absolute and desirable goals. Absolute goals are the essential ones, while desirable goals are important but not indispensable.

4. *Compile a priority listing for the desirable goals.* Do this by asking all the people who will be involved with the goals to give their opinions on their relative importance.

Use this information to help you rate the goals and decide on priorities. You might use a simple number system—from 1 to 10, for example. Again, ask when these goals should be completed. Do you have the manpower and material to achieve them?

Don't always measure the goals in dollars and cents or in production quotas. Think about such criteria as company image, growth potential, etc. You might find that some goals place limits on others, so trade-offs will be necessary. The priority listing will guide you in your choices.

WARNING: Don't set too many goals for your department. Emery maintains that few individuals can work effectively toward more than five challenging high-priority goals a year. Teams can handle more, but not more than ten to twelve, he estimates. Emery counsels managers to "*reduce* rather than expand the number of team goals" in any final listing.

2. GET ALL
THE FACTS

Problem: Where Does the Problem Lie?

"I don't understand why production has been down lately," George Freedley, production manager of a clothing manufacturing plant, said to his assistant, Rochelle Goldstein. They were discussing a recent memo from the vice-president of the firm.

"The problem as I see it has to do with the fact that material has been arriving late at the plant," Rochelle volunteered.

"How do you know that's true? Have you talked to the purchasing agents? Have they complained to suppliers?" Freedley asked.

"Well, not exactly. I was just repeating something I heard through the grapevine," Rochelle admitted sheepishly.

* * * * *

Step 2: Get All the Facts

Don't make assumptions about where the problem or problems lie. Find out for yourself or assign your staff to find out. The first major step in problem solving is to get all the facts. The manager has to know not only what information is available but also where to get that information and how best to use it.

Talk to the people directly involved, and even those not so directly involved. Find out if others have encountered the same or similar problems, and study how they handled it. Read about the issues. Investigate the history of the problem area. You should, if possible, have access to outside consultants who can help you understand the situation. Or, somebody on your staff might fulfill this need. The point is to get more than one view on the problem.

As you gather the facts, you will find, in many cases, that your initial perception of the problem was wrong. In the case mentioned at the beginning of the chapter, Freedley tracked the problem down by talking to purchasing agents and suppliers and then checking delivery receipts against inventory records; and he found that supplies were *not* arriving late. Rather, a shortage of workers in the unloading area was delaying the unloading process and creating the snag in production.

Remember that formulating the right problem is at least as important as finding the right solution. The following are some questions that you should ask as you and your staff play the role of reporters ferreting out the facts. Make sure to get the facts rather than opinions or speculation. And whenever possible, have those facts corroborated by others familiar with the problem.

How to Get Background on the Problem

1. *Find out who made the original complaint, and pinpoint the circumstances surrounding it.* Emery suggests that you ask

questions along these lines: When did they first notice the problem? Did others notice what was happening? How did they first notice the problem? In addition, he advises that you ferret out the answers to these crucial and related questions: "Are we missing any useful information here, and are we sure that this information is accurate?"

2. *Trace the events that brought about the present situation.* Question all those involved. Be particularly sensitive to any recent change that might account for the difficulty. Can anybody locate a specific factor that might have caused the difficulty? For instance, you may find that a minor change in procedures had an unexpectedly large and negative impact.

3. *Identify all the factors contributing to the problem—as well as those helping to control it.* Once you have found the trouble spot, isolate the related factors that might be exacerbating it. Think in terms of two questions raised by Auren Uris in *The Executive Deskbook*: What factors intensify the difficulty, and which ones alleviate it?

4. *Periodically ask yourself, "Does this involve any deeper issues?"* In some cases, problems will be interconnected through a chain of cause and effect. You may recognize a problem, analyze it, and find its cause—and then find yourself asking, "How did the cause come into being?" Thus, the cause becomes a new problem to be analyzed and explained, and its cause may, in turn, become yet another problem for study and solution.

5. *Find out the scope of the problem.* Michael Sanderson, in *Successful Problem Management*, suggests that you ask such questions as: Is this problem larger than you imagined? Who is affected by it? Is everybody affected the same way? What areas are affected? Is the problem contained in one area, or among one group of workers? Will this problem require a minor adjustment or a comprehensive change? And finally, Sanderson urges that problem solvers think in terms of this central question: "Can the problem be broken up into subproblems which can fairly safely be dealt with separately?"

6. *Identify the time period involved.* When was the problem first noticed? Had it been developing before then—and for how long? Has it been quietly developing over a long period, or did

it flare up unexpectedly? Is this problem permanent, or can we wait for it to fade away?

7. *Try to identify the growth, change, or evolutionary pattern of the problem.* Has it been developing in cycles? Does it always appear in the same place? What internal forces might be affecting that growth? What external factors—business cycles, economic trends, etc.—might be affecting its growth?

8. *Avoid labels.* Don't lump together related problems, and don't confuse the symptoms with the problem. For instance, you might characterize a worker problem as a morale issue, and leave it at that. Such an approach would oversimplify the issues. A morale problem, in fact, might include a variety of problems, all of which have to be dealt with in their particular fashion. For example, it might include such problems as: 1) high turnover; 2) an increase in grievances among workers; 3) a communication problem between workers and supervisors; 4) problems with a new recreation facility—or any number of other issues that might affect morale.

9. *Question whatever assumptions you or others have made about the problem.* Are those assumptions correct? Do you have the background facts to substantiate them? What do your staff, co-workers, rank-and-file employees, and consultants feel about those assumptions? Ask yourself if those assumptions might not be getting in the way of a clear understanding of what is happening.

WARNING: Be wary about accepting anything at face value. As Russell L. Ackoff says in *The Art of Problem Solving*: "The more obvious . . . a fact appears, the more intensely its truth should be investigated." We are much more likely to be wrong about what we accept without evidence, Ackoff notes, than in what we accept with evidence—even if that evidence seems unlikely.

3. ANALYZE THE PROBLEM

Problem: What to Do With All This Information?

Jack Monaghan, managing editor of the *Long Island Daily*, sat behind his desk, staring at his notes. Troubled by a rash of typos and transposed lines in the paper, Monaghan had done some sleuthing to find out where the problem originated. "Was it connected to the computerized equipment, or did the problem have to do with the staff—the copy editors, keyboarders or proofreaders?" he wanted to know. He felt confident that he had done his research thoroughly as he looked over his notes. But now he had to move on to the next step in his investigation. "What should I do with all this information?" he asked himself. "How do I analyze what I have found?"

* * * * *

Step 3: Analyze the Problem

It is certainly true that a problem clearly stated is already half solved. But it is also true, as Charles H. Kepner and Benjamin B. Tregoe note in *The Rational Manager*, "that a problem cannot be efficiently solved unless it is precisely described." Analyzing the problem by breaking it down into its component pieces will help you isolate the source of the problem—and "precisely describe" what has happened.

Some problems, of course, don't require a very detailed approach. But for complicated or difficult problems, a detailed analysis and precise description of the deviation is necessary.

Sometimes you may find yourself approaching the problem in the same way time after time, only to reach the same dead end. Try using a variety of techniques to get different perspectives on the issue. While you are doing this, be sure to consult with others to get their views. Discuss the problem with your boss, with your subordinates, with the rank-and-file employees directly involved, with specialists on and off your staff, and with people who may have no direct connection with the problem. Alternative viewpoints—a cross-fertilization of ideas —can prove invaluable. Conflict of opinion, as Helen Reynolds and Mary E. Tramel advise in *Executive Time Management*, should be used to explore all major aspects of important problems.

How to Analyze the Problem

1. *Find the "critical dimensions" of the problem by analyzing it from four perspectives—identity, location, time, and extent.* This method of analysis is suggested by Kepner and Tregoe in *The Rational Manager*. The point is to draw a boundary line around the problem by sharply separating what the problem *is* from what it *is not*. The sharper the dividing line between what is and is not the problem, note Kepner and Tregoe, the easier it is to find the desired clues to cause.

   • Begin by writing down *what* the deviation is. Limit your description to a sentence or phrase. Under that, state the object, person, group, process, or anything else affected by the deviation. To make the

description more precise, you must distinguish between what the problem *is* and what it *is not*. So, in a
column parallel to the *is* column, write those things
or conditions that are a part of the problem area but
have not been affected by the deviation.

- State precisely *where* the deviation occurs on the object,
  process, etc., and where the objects were observed.
  Then note the items unaffected by the deviation.
- Write down *when* the deviation appears, as well as
  those periods when it did not occur. This step iso-
  lates the time frame for the problem.
- State the *extent* or size. Here, you might also report
  how many objects have been observed in this deviation. In the *is not* column, note the area or areas
  unaffected by the deviation.

Using this method of analysis, Jack Monaghan, in the
case described at the beginning of the chapter, could draw certain conclusions and focus on certain aspects of the problem.
For example, the data would indicate that the problem stems
from not the editorial but the production side of the paper.
Since the deviation occurs mainly in late news stories and he
knows that news sections are put together under tighter deadlines than the feature sections, he might begin to suspect that
deadlines play a large role in the problem. He might start to
question procedures for laying out late-breaking news stories
that go into the afternoon edition. Noting that the problem first
surfaced in April, Monaghan might recall that the production
department went on a new schedule in March. In short, several
areas of inquiry would be opened up by this method of analysis.
    2. *Try dividing the problem or any information about it into its
distinguishable parts.* This approach is suggested by K.F. Jackson
in *The Art of Solving Problems*. Jackson advises that you take the
problem apart and examine each part or item well enough to
describe it in detail. It might be helpful to put down on paper
what you have discovered. After breaking down the problem

into its components, state how the parts relate to each other and how they mesh as a whole. Have you recognized any new relationships between the parts? Do you now understand what is going on? If not, ask yourself, "What is missing from the picture?"

3. *Try looking at the problem from a completely different perspective.* Michael Sanderson recommends this technique in *Successful Problem Management.* Ask yourself how the situation would look if you had a different role in the organization. Or, instead of looking at the problem as a producer, try seeing it through the eyes of the retailer. Or go even further. Look at related examples from completely unrelated fields. Perhaps, you can compare the losing performance of your sales team with the losing performance of your favorite football team. In this case, you might notice that you rely too much on a "star performer" who isn't always dependable, or that "your team" begins the season well but loses momentum quickly.

4. *Draw a map or picture of the different pieces of the problem.* Sanderson suggests this technique as a way to find how each piece of the puzzle is connected to the other—and how it could or should be connected. Are there missing pieces? How can you make connections between those missing parts? A rough sketch should emerge of what is joined to what, why and how, as Sanderson puts it.

5. *Use a chain diagram.* This technique may provide you with a clearer idea of what is happening, K.F. Jackson says. Simply lay out all the elements of the problem in sequence. Next to the key word that identifies who or what is involved at that stage, state what you have discovered about the problem. For instance, take the example of the sales director of a shoe manufacturing firm who is trying to track down a recurrent problem of late deliveries to customers. This sales director might set up the diagram along the lines shown on page 24.

6. *Use numbers to help understand a problem.* In *The Executive Deskbook,* Auren Uris suggests that numbers are helpful in such areas as gauging employee performance. Suppose an employee's performance involves four main functions. Assign a

Chain Diagram

Elements of Problem　　　　　**Your Findings**

Manufacturer

Transportation

Wholesaler

Transportation

Retailer

weight to each of these functions, reflecting their importance to the organization. You might decide to assign function A a value of 40 percent, while the other three functions each receive 20 percent. Then evaluate the quality of that employee's performance in each of those functions, keeping in mind that achievements or failures in function A count twice as much as those in each of the other three functions.

7. Take a break if you find yourself going around in circles. Give the ideas a chance to incubate in your mind. Also, remember to schedule your problem solving during periods when you feel most creative—and open to ideas. We all have high and low points in our daily energy cycle.

WARNING: Bring an open mind to problem analysis. Make sure you are not unconsciously fitting the facts to your particular bias. There is always a tendency to find the facts that one is looking for, but be aware of this tendency and resist it.

4. EVALUATE THE CONSEQUENCES

Problem: To Act or Not to Act?

It was approaching six o'clock, and Kurt Jenkins looked nervously at his watch and then back at the progress report on his desk. Jenkins, vice-president of operations at Delphi Tools, was wrestling with a problem that had preoccupied him all day. A few months earlier, under pressure from the union, Delphi had changed its assembly-line procedures. Instead of employees working on only one step of production, each was now given a chance to do more than one job on the assembly line. It seemed a good solution to a growing morale problem at the plant—worker apathy that was undermining production quotas and schedules.

But now Jenkins felt an increasing sense of alarm. The report indicated that the changeover had not gone smoothly: some of the workers were having trouble adapting to their new jobs. Perhaps the problem is only temporary, he tried to console himself. "Should I act now, and suggest that we go back to the old system, or wait and see how things develop?" he asked himself for the hundredth time that day.

*   *   *   *   *

Step 4. Evaluate the Consequences

Whether to act or not is one of the first and most important things to consider once you have completed your research and analysis of the problem. Sometimes it is better to let a situation work itself out; to interfere runs the risk of making it worse. One must always weigh the effort and risk of action against the risk of inaction.

Jenkins has one obvious first step to take: he should involve assembly-line workers in his deliberations on whether to stay with the new procedures or return to the old system. If worker apathy was one of the causes for the changeover, more, not less, worker participation in problem analysis and decision making seems in order.

How serious is the deviation and what is its potential for growth? These are the issues to be weighed when deciding whether to act. There is no surefire way of making this decision, but Peter F. Drucker offers good advice: "Act if on balance the benefits greatly outweigh the cost and risk."

What follows are a list of questions to ask when weighing whether to act and with what degree of urgency. The questions are adapted from those in Sanderson's *Successful Problem Management* and Jackson's *The Art of Solving Problems*.

How to Evaluate Consequences

1. *Study the trend of the problem and its potential for growth.* Does the problem look as if it will burn itself out and disappear, or will it grow progressively worse? What has happened before in similar cases? What has been its rate of growth, and will it continue at that rate? Is that growth contained, or does it offer the potential of spreading to other areas?

2. *Consider the long-term effects of this problem.* Can you live with this change? How will it affect other departments or your

resources? Will it lead to shortages in material or stresses on manpower? How will it affect goals and intervening quotas? How will it affect the image or policies of the organization? Can the personnel involved handle it without disrupting procedures? If not, you must consider what kind of resources will be allocated to the problem. If it looks like a serious problem, make sure you know exactly how serious.

3. *Find out if this is part of a normal business cycle or a symptom of a larger problem.* Study the outside forces influencing the problem—the effects of competition, fluctuations in the market, state of the economy, personnel changes, etc. How do all these factors influence the problem and its development?

4. *Learn whether the problem represents a safety problem now or in the immediate future.* If an accident occurs, is it an isolated event, or should it be taken as proof that something is intrinsically wrong with the system? What about the safeguards being used—should they be reexamined and strengthened?

WARNING: Be careful to distinguish between a legitimate urgency for reaching a solution as opposed to emotional pressures influencing your judgment. For example, don't rush into a dramatic solution simply because you want to impress your superiors or co-workers. Acting out of superficial and self-serving motives can lead to shortsighted and possibly disastrous policies.

5. MAP A GENERAL STRATEGY

Problem: How Should I Handle This Problem?

"What should I do?" Harvey Gold asked his associate, Andrew Kalb. The two executives were considering how to respond to reports of a malfunction in a small group of radios produced at the plant.

"I know that so far the problem has been isolated to one area of the operation," Gold said. "At least, I feel we have it under control, although we haven't really started working on it yet," he continued. "The problem is that I feel too pressured right now, and so does the rest of the staff—with inventory coming up—so I don't feel I can give the problem my best attention." He paused, adding, "Nor do I feel the problem has to be dealt with immediately."

"Well, have you considered taking some kind of interim action, to make sure the problem doesn't get worse?" Kalb suggested. "Then you can work on a solution at a more leisurely pace."

*   *   *   *   *

Step 5: Map a General Strategy

Kalb's suggestion is sound. Harvey Gold should devise an interim solution, and then take the time to develop a more comprehensive one. This interim move might involve more careful monitoring at the plant so that malfunctions are identified and isolated early. The point is to realize before you begin developing alternatives that several courses of action are open to you.

Now that you know something about the nature of the problem, you should map out a general strategy. For instance, you might decide that the solution you are looking for now may not be the final one; it may simply keep the problem from spreading while you and your staff develop a solution that eliminates the problem. You might also decide after investigating the problem that you will have to live with it—at least for a while—and see how you can adapt to it in the best possible way. On many problems, it is necessary to take successively both interim and corrective action.

The following are five courses of action open to you.

How to Map a General Strategy

1. *Decide to take a policy of corrective action if the problem is urgent and risks serious consequences.* This is an action that eliminates the deviation by eliminating the cause. You have been moved to take this action by the urgency of the problem and its potential for growth. This is the most effective action, although any number of pressures may prevent you from taking it.

2. *Take interim action if you need time to develop a comprehensive solution.* This interim action, it is hoped, will provide a stopgap solution that paves the way for a corrective decision. In this case, you believe the problem is not so urgent that you can't delay making a final decision. For example, you might not be able to find the right person to fill a job slot, so you decide to

rotate people in that position until you find the right individual.
3. *Take adaptive action if you can live with the problem*. Either you have found that you can do nothing to eliminate the cause or else feel that any real action would be too risky. You have decided, then, to live with the problem—and hope to minimize its effects.
4. *Take a preventive course if you foresee a problem developing*. Good, methodical management will help you recognize a potential trouble spot and take action that averts the problem.
5. *Take contingency action if you have tried one plan only to see it fail*. Always try to have contingency plans in reserve. As an example, you might have arranged for a speaker to talk before your business group, only to discover at the last minute that your guest speaker cannot make it. If you have had the foresight to line up a substitute, you needn't worry about your original plan falling through.

WARNING: Act decisively, no matter what course of action you decide on. Don't hedge: a reluctance to face the problem squarely can create only more problems. The effective decision maker, Drucker notes in *The Effective Executive*, "either acts or he doesn't act. He does not take half-actions."

PART 2: Working with alternatives

Before rushing into a solution, you must decide what exactly you want to accomplish and what resources you have to work with. Once you know where you want to go, start brainstorming ways of getting there. Which leads to the next phase of this decision-making process: sifting through the alternatives to find the one that best fits the bill. Begin by getting an effective decision-making team together...

6. ORGANIZE A DECISION-MAKING TEAM

Problem: Working It Out With Your Staff

"Didn't you work with Patrick O'Hanlon or any of the other line supervisors when you were making your decision?" Stewart Halprin shook his head at Tom Matthew's question. Halprin, production manager of a tool-and-die company, had recently instituted a stepped-up production schedule at the plant, only to discover that the new schedule had run into immediate resistance. "I think if you had worked with O'Hanlon or any of the other fellows down at the plant, you would have realized that the quotas were unrealistic," Matthews, vice-president of the company, said. "A lot of new men are being broken in at the present time, and this is slowing things down temporarily."

"I would have liked to have worked closer with the people down at the plant, but I was under pressure to act quickly," Halprin said. "Unfortunately, there's no way of working out the decision with the guys down there without wasting a lot of time in meetings. And I just couldn't afford that time," he concluded.

*　　*　　*　　*　　*

Step 6: Organize a Decision-Making Team

Halprin was shortsighted to feel that a cooperative decision-making effort would have taken too much time. Managers should involve their subordinates whenever possible during the problem-solving and decision-making period. In fact, the trend now in industry is toward fuller cooperation by employees at all levels of the company. Inspired by the example of the Japanese, more and more American companies are experimenting with what is sometimes called "consensus management." A marked departure from the traditional top-to-bottom form of hierarchical management, consensus management involves giving workers a larger role in setting the goals and standards on the shop floor. This may be done through "Quality Circles," where worker representatives work directly in committee groups with managers to analyze problems and suggest improvements.

How to Develop a Decision Team

1. *Get your staff together to discuss and identify the problems involved and the purpose of the decision.* At this meeting, you should come to a basic understanding of what will be the main goal of your decision. If the meeting drags on, cut it short and advise those with more ideas on the subject to put their thoughts in writing.

2. *Develop a Factor Review Task Force to work closely with you on developing the decision.* This group, David A. Emery suggests in *The Compleat Manager*, might be elected by your staff in the first meeting, or appointed by you. One of its jobs will be to help you decide the main requirements or criteria of your decision. This group should convene periodically to work with you as you develop your criteria, brainstorm ideas, evaluate alternatives, and make a final choice. At the same time, this group will work with those who might be affected by the decision, and with

people within the company who may have input into the problem.

3. *Consult outside experts.* They can help you to understand what is happening, and to recognize flaws in your analysis. Many management experts stress the importance of having outside authorities or consultants during problem solving and decision making. These outside experts may prove particularly valuable when you are faced with choosing between alternatives for your final decision.

4. *Include a balance of talents in your decision-making team.* For example, have on tap both long-range and short-range thinkers; practical and creative thinkers; those adept in mathematical logic and those possessing a creative and non-linear style.

5. *Be open-minded and encouraging even when you disagree with your subordinates' views.* If you want more creative decisions, show subordinates that you will not judge them harshly if they make a mistake. Otherwise, they will tend to make "safe" decisions or no decisions at all, warn Oxenfeldt, Miller, and Dickinson in *A Basic Approach to Executive Decision Making.*

6. *Make sure your staff understands the goals and objectives you are working toward.* All the staff members should play a role in defining them.

7. *Foster a feeling of equality and cooperation at decision-making meetings.* Don't allow certain members of the group to dominate the meeting.

8. *Don't rush to criticize ideas that seem offbeat or wrong-headed.* Study them, perhaps twist them around, evaluate them in a different light, or extrapolate from them to see if there isn't something usable.

9. *Curb decision-making blocks in yourself and in members of your team.* Auren Uris, in *The Executive Deskbook*, identifies some of the psychological blocks that can prevent a manager from being a good decision maker. Among the problems:

• *Hamlet syndrome.* Like Shakespeare's Hamlet, some people are unable to come to a decision without excessive hand-wringing. In many cases, their indecisiveness stems from fear: that their choice may not be wise and that the consequences of a less-than-perfect decision may prove disastrous. A good antidote to these fears is to take a can-do attitude, say management experts. Psychologists have proven time after time that the individual who is optimistic about problem solving stands a better chance of success than someone who approaches the problem pessimistically. Also remember that an effective decision maker is prepared for any kind of contingency.

• *Compulsiveness.* Some individuals have the opposite problem of the "Hamlet disease": they are too quick to make decisions. These are the people who jump before looking. They feel compelled to make decisions. A good way to counteract this tendency is simply to proceed with problem solving and decision making in the systematic way suggested in this book. Taking the time to understand the problem and analyze the choices available for your decision will bridle the tendency to make snap decisions. Working with others, getting their feedback and suggestions, will also curb the urge to shoot from the hip.

• *Do-nothing tendency.* This is a variant of the Hamlet syndrome, except that these victims lull themselves into a false sense of security—and do nothing. Believing that the situation will work itself out in time without outside intervention is often a shortcut to disaster. Sometimes it *is* better to do nothing. But before shrugging one's shoulders and walking away, one should fully explore the potential consequences.

WARNING: Be sensitive to your workers' needs, but don't become immobilized by the fear of making an unpopular decision. Sometimes the right decision might involve layoffs or personnel changes that cause hardship. Make sure that your concern for others doesn't lead to "consequence anxiety." The right decision may be initially unpopular but beneficial to the majority in the long run. The crucial thing is to let those affected share in the problem-solving and decision-making process so they will understand your final choice.

7. DEVELOP CRITERIA

Problem: Getting the Priorities Straight

"I really can't devote too much time to looking for new offices at this point," Ellen Steiner, head of a New York clothing design firm, remarked to her head designer, Michael Northrup. "But we should move within the next couple of months before we start working at full speed on our summer line. We can't let this whole moving process delay work on our summerwear."

"The thing is that I really haven't decided where our new offices should be," Steiner said. "It would be nice to have them in the Village, not far from where I live. On the other hand, I don't know if we could afford the rents there. Maybe we should stay in the garment center, so we're right in the middle of things," she continued. "Well, I guess I'll make up my mind when I see what's available."

Step 7: Develop Your Criteria

Before even considering alternatives—in this case looking at office space—you must have your requirements clearly in mind. You cannot make an intelligent choice until you know precisely where you want to end up. Now you must define the specifications for your decision. If you fail to understand what these are, you run the risk of developing a solution that has been put together to justify a foregone conclusion—which may be the wrong conclusion.

We will refer to these specifications as the "criteria" for your decision, using John D. Arnold's term from *The Art of Decision Making*. The more exact the fit between your criteria and your final decision, the better the likelihood is that you have made the right choice. At the same time, drawing up a list of criteria for your decision will lead you into the search for alternative solutions. Use the list as your blueprint. Study it, and think of solutions that fit the specifications of this blueprint. And then after developing your alternatives, measure each one against this set of criteria, in order to see how well each alternative fulfills these requirements. As Emery notes in *The Compleat Manager*, a clear definition of your criteria "should be the basis of every significant choice of alternatives."

Work closely with your staff. It is helpful to put down your ideas in the form of a checklist. This checklist will be your road map as you develop alternatives and then evaluate them.

How to Define Your Criteria

1. *Begin by asking yourself repeatedly: What is/should be/could be happening?*" This question is suggested by Arnold in *The Art of Decision Making*. As Arnold notes, the gap between "what is happening" and "what should be happening" will start you thinking about what your decision must achieve. "What is," of course, deals with the situation as it is presently. "What should be" refers to our expectations—what past history and experience have led us to expect. "What could be," however, takes us one step further. Instead of settling for a remedial solution, we set our sights higher by thinking about the best that could happen. Making the leap from "what should be happening" to "what could be happening" will start you thinking about the kind of results that a really creative solution would achieve.

2. *Write a brief statement of purpose.* As Oxenfeldt et al. note in *A Basic Approach to Executive Decision Making*, one should always start with an initial statement of objectives. Begin by stating in one or two sentences what you want accomplished. Think about what you decided "could be happening," and try to incorporate that goal into your statement of purpose. Choose something manageable and positive, and express it as an opportunity. At the beginning, the best approach is to state the purpose in broad terms. Arnold maintains that formulation of this statement is the most critical, yet most often neglected, step in the decision-making process. Many people jump into a search for solutions without clarifying what they want to accomplish. The results: shortsighted and unimaginative solutions.

3. *Write specific objectives that would achieve the goal described in your statement of purpose.* Start thinking now in concrete terms. Think about this question, posed by Kepner and Tregoe: "What returns do we want for our efforts?" For instance, a manager intent on increasing profits should be precise about this objective. What kind of profits? How much? Where? When? What kind of changes will it, and should it, bring? Be sure also to keep in mind the goals of the company—the standards and policies that helped you detect the problem in the first place. You are now beginning to develop what Arnold terms the criteria for your eventual decision.

4. *Determine what the decision must preserve.* After deciding what you would like to see happen, think about what should remain unchanged. Suppose you want to computerize your mail-order business but not change your staff. This desire to maintain your present staff will then be a criterion for your decision. Or, in the example at the beginning of the chapter, Steiner might decide that the new office space should require no more than minor renovations. At the same time, Drucker reminds us, we should not forget to reexamine our assumptions about what we want to remain unchanged; perhaps, we have grown to accept some part of the operation that really should be changed.

5. *Ask yourself what the decision should help avoid.* Steiner might, for example, want the location to be convenient to all the

staff. Convenience, then, becomes a criterion. The last offices had no elevator, and clients had to climb three flights of stairs, she might recall. And so this time, the office should be in an elevator building.

6. *When considering a new product, think in terms of "end-user requirements."* Emery defines these as the requirements of those who use the product—often the customer. Are you thinking specifically about the needs of this end-user, and how that individual or firm will use the product? Questions include: How will the product provide for adequate comfort and maximum safety? How should it improve on what is currently on the market? What should be the cost requirements? How will it provide for maximum utility? Answers to these questions and others will be reflected in your criteria.

How to Decide Priorities

Armed with your list of what the decision should accomplish, you may now establish priorities for these criteria—decide the relative importance of all the requirements you have established for the decision. Not all of these criteria will be of equal importance. What you must do is divide them into two groups, based roughly on their relative importance to the final decision. Arnold suggests that these two groups be categorized as the "absolute requirements" and the "desirable objectives"; Kepner and Tregoe, offering a similar weighting system, divide the two groups into "musts" and "wants."

Whatever the terms you decide to use, the important thing is to arrange these criteria—these specifications—into a hierarchy of importance, so that later you will be better able to evaluate the alternatives by measuring them against these criteria. Eventually, you will pare down your choices and make trade-offs. Decisions on trade-offs will be easier when you know the relative value of a criterion. (For sample list of criteria, see page 42.)

At the same time, you should remember that these criteria must not only meet the needs of the decision at hand but also should reflect the long-range goals and intervening objectives of your department as well as your organization (see Step 1). The objectives of all analysis in decision making "should always balance and harmonize the immediate and long-range future" of an organization, as Drucker notes in *The Practice of Management*.

The following are guidelines to ranking the priority of your criteria.

1. *Decide which criteria are indispensable to the solution.* Ask this question suggested by Arnold: "Which criteria are so important that no solution is acceptable unless it meets all of them?" These are what Arnold calls the "absolute requirements" of the decision. Analyze why this objective is essential. Hold a meeting of your Factor Review Task Force (see p. 34) to see if the members of the group agree with your opinion. Ask yourself if it is possible to construct a solution without fulfilling this requirement.

2. *Evaluate the remaining criteria in terms of their value to the solution.* Again, do this ranking with your Factor Review Task Force and seek a consensus of opinion. Use a simple ranking of 1 to 10, the 10 for those criteria that are the most important but not indispensable. The first step in this weighting process, say Kepner and Tregoe, is to establish "the position of each WANT objective with relation to the next." This is done, they add, by giving it a numerical weight of importance. The criteria assigned a value of 10 becomes the standard by which we measure the less important criteria. At the other end of the spectrum, give a rating of 1 to the least important criteria. The same ranking can go to more than one criterion. If you have trouble establishing the values, Arnold as well as Kepner and Tregoe suggest that you ask yourself such questions as: Why is this important? What would be lost if it weren't a criterion? What other criteria are less/more important than this one? The ranked list then becomes what Arnold calls the "desirable objectives" and Kepner and Tregoe call the "wants."

Sample List of Criteria for Decision Making

After discussing the issues with the staff and evaluating their needs and those of the company, Ellen Steiner drew up a list of criteria to direct them in their search for new office space. Her statement of purpose is: Determine the best space available for the company and the employees.

Absolute Requirements		Desirable Objectives
Office must be in	10	Light, airy space
Manhattan	10	Occupancy as soon as possible
Safe building	10	Elevator building
Less than $3,000 a	9	1,200 square feet or more
month	8	In or near the garment center
Convenient to subways	8	Available for three-year lease
and buses	7	Recently renovated building
Minor renovations	5	Superintendent on premises
	5	Facilities for cooking
	5	Separate office area along with large work area

WARNING: Don't be too cautious at too early a stage. Later you will have to scale down your thinking to fit constraints of time, money, etc. It is better now to be bold and imaginative. Drucker advises managers "to start with what is right rather than with what is acceptable," since compromise is inevitable in the end.

8. IDENTIFY RESOURCES

Problem: Do We Have the Resources?

"Right away, I liked the idea. In fact, I've already started investigating this market," Nick Langione declared to his sales director, Alex Verrastro. Langione, market manager for an Italian-American food company, was discussing a suggestion made by their ad agency that they think about adding frozen meatball hero sandwiches as a way to diversify their product line.

"It's an interesting idea," Verrastro replied, "but let's think for a second about what we have to work with. Do we have the resources to shift into frozen food production? The change could prove expensive. Maybe we can come up with another way of diversifying while using our existing resources."

* * * * *

Step 8: Identify Resources

An early step in the search for alternatives is to determine what resources you can draw on to carry out a decision. Work closely with your staff to find out what is available.

The manager should have a checklist of resources as a guide. K.F. Jackson, in *The Art of Solving Problems*, suggests that you think in terms of the 3M's—money, material, and manpower—when defining those resources. When possible, break down the resources into categories.

The following checklist is compiled from a variety of management experts. Evaluate your resources in terms of availability, quantity, and quality.

How to Identify Resources

1. *Determine your manpower supply.* Think about manpower in terms of both skill and numbers. Do you have people to whom you can delegate authority confidently? Do your workers have the competence and flexibility to adapt to a major change in procedures or production? If you need more personnel, where will you find them? Can you draw on people with special talents?

2. *Define your cost limitations.* Before spinning out an ambitious solution, pinpoint the money at your disposal. What returns can you expect? Where will you get more money if you need it? And how big a consideration should money be in this case?

3. *Identify the kind of material you can draw on.* What are the facilities available, and can they be expanded? What raw materials are at your disposal—in terms of quantity and quality?

4. *Consider how much influence your organization's policies, image, and goals should have on your decision.* For example, you might refer to the organization's hiring policies before making personnel changes. A policy of hiring from within would, of course, influence your thinking. Or, the company might have to fill EEO quotas. The organizational structure and command hierarchy might also shape the direction of your thinking.

5. *Examine whether you have the resources to meet production*

goals. Are the quantities in the goals reasonable? Should you accept the goals as hard-and-fast guidelines? At the same time, ask yourself about quality requirements. How would your decision improve the quality of work, working conditions, product, or company image, and so on?

6. *Analyze the external as well as internal factors that will affect resources.* An array of factors could influence the direction of your thinking: economic trends, competition, sales pattern of the company, government regulation, role played by unions in your business, legal complications, consumer and industry attitudes, etc. Not all problems involve such a wide range of influences and complications, yet many problems that seem simple on the surface involve an intricate web of factors.

7. *Locate sources of help in your search for solutions.* Are there specialists within the organization to help you? Can you draw on other sources of information and practical help—books, magazines, outside authorities—as you develop solutions? Have you gone to the right people to find out what is happening?

8. *Examine your time limitations.* Will you have enough time to achieve an ambitious and long-range solution? Or should you think now about an interim solution, which will provide breathing room until you can come up with a more comprehensive solution.

WARNING: Be sure that you thoroughly understand the policies and procedures of your organization, since the right decision may require a deviation from accepted practice. Think through what you want to change and why. Otherwise, you fall prey to the dilemma of "trying at one and the same time both to alter and preserve established practice," as Drucker warns.

9. BRAINSTORM CREATIVE ALTERNATIVES

Problem: "This Problem Has Me Stumped!"

"This problem has me stumped," Marketing Manager David Reed complained to his sales director, Ken Grant. In the last two years, their machine tool company had been buffeted by a sales cycle that had played havoc with their production quotas. When the economy was on an upswing, sales of the product soared. But as soon as there was a downturn, sales took a nose dive.

"I think we can take advantage of the problem," Grant suggested. "We may simply have to live with irregular demand, but what we can do is diversify our products. We should look for a new product that has a demand cycle counter to that of the machine tools but would involve a similar technology."

*   *   *   *   *

Step 9: Cast a Wide Net for New Ideas

Ken Grant's suggestion shows he was thinking along creative lines—visualizing how to turn a problem into an opportunity. You have already laid the groundwork for your decision making by developing the criteria for evaluating your alternatives. At this point, it is best to move away from straightforward analysis and let your imagination take over—to help develop creative solutions. Open up your thinking, liberate it from constraints, cast a wide net for ideas. Brainstorming can provide insights that lead to new, and possibly innovative, solutions.

What follows are some of the methods proposed by management experts to spin off ideas. These ideas, in turn, may form the basis of the alternatives from which you will derive a solution. Most of these methods can and should be done with either another person or a group, so that a wide range of possibilities are explored. It is important to investigate every possibility—even if it seems farfetched. As Michael Sanderson says in *Successful Problem Management*, try to "juggle, juxtapose and fantasize" to generate as many ideas as possible.

Sanderson and other management experts advise keeping an idea bank. This might be just a folder of clippings, notes, and pamphlets. For a plant manager, it might include a shelf of catalogs for equipment and materials. An advertising executive might have folders of clippings about products related to an account, articles dealing with popular tastes and buying trends, and old advertisements.

Analogy

Looking for an *analogy*, or likeness, to your problem in totally unrelated areas may provide unexpected insights. History is filled with examples of scientists and inventors who made their discoveries through creative analogy. Gutenberg, for example, saw an analogy between the winepress and printing, and the result was a revolution in communications.

HOW TO USE ANALOGY

1. *Think of an inanimate object from everyday life—such as a household appliance—that performs a function similar to what you*

want to achieve. Let that object serve as your model. Or take randomly selected objects—a button, a hinge, a wheel, etc.— and think how its form or function might illuminate the problem at hand. Study the mechanism, mentally twist it around, break it into its separate parts—and think how it might suggest a new approach to your problem.

2. *Choose an example from nature as your model for creative analogy*. Does the form or function of a plant or animal provide the principle for a solution? This use of nature as a launching pad for new ideas and solutions is called *Bionics*. It has been used with success in science and industry. For example, study of the beetle's eye led to the development of a superior ground-speed indicator for aircraft.

Synectics

Synectics is one of the most popular methods, particularly with groups, to stimulate creative problem solving. As described by George Prince in *The Practice of Creativity*, synectics helps to release the conscious mind from its inhibitions by first forcing it to focus away from, and then allowing it to return to, the problem. Synectics relies on the unrestricted use of metaphor and analogy. Two basic activities constitute the approach. First, the problem is pulled apart and analyzed to "make the strange familiar," according to Oxenfeldt et al. Second, the process is reversed—to "make the familiar strange."

HOW TO USE THE SYNECTICS METHOD

1. *Analyze the problem*. During the first part of the group synectics sessions, decide on your objectives.

2. *Move far afield to generate analogies*. Free associate. Take examples from everyday life. For example, the behavior of a tornado may come under scrutiny during a brainstorming session, representing a natural force with great suction power and a predictable pattern of behavior.

3. *Now develop a book title, a two-word phrase, that captures the paradoxical nature of this force.* "Controlled Fury" might be one title for the analogy. The group follows the same method to examine other analogies. These "excursions," as Prince calls them, loosen up the thinking of the group while forcing the participants to search widely through their own experiences. The book title distills their thinking into a handy phrase that might suggest a principle applicable to the problem.

4. *Extrapolate from the analogy to the problem.* The group asks itself what new ideas the analogy offers for approaching the problem.

The idea is to let the mind wander away from predictable paths. The disadvantage of conventional thinking, Prince notes, is that "the mind is a skillful pigeonholer." It must break out of its limitations to reach its imaginative potential.

Brainstorming in Action

A good example of brainstorming in action is offered by George M. Prince in *The Practice of Creativity*. In this case, a group of executives uses an analogy from nature as a creative springboard to come up with a new way of handling a problem with their boss.

The problem: a senior executive at their company tends to react negatively to the ideas of others. Five junior executives want to make this executive aware of the fact that he does not respond constructively to their ideas—without antagonizing him.

Casting about through analogies in nature while using the synectics technique, they try to zero in on a natural force that exhibits a principle relevant to their situation: an elemental force with the ability to move large objects in a gentle and gradual way. After spinning off a variety of possibilities, they come up with the idea of *erosion*. But how, they ask, can erosion be adapted to this particular circumstance? One group member suggests that they must wear their boss down; another executive points out that erosion is a collective force.

This idea inspires another member of the group to suggest that the five of them propose the same idea, but each in a different fashion, so that they wear down the boss's resistance. They would encourage him to comment constructively, not dismiss the ideas out of hand. This idea is thrown around, until one of the executives gives it a final refinement. The first person, after presenting the idea and hearing the senior executive's criticism, will ask for his suggestions on how the idea can be improved. The procedure is then repeated, with the next person proposing the initial idea, which now incorporates the boss's suggestions. If the boss uses sarcasm, they will simply ask how he can improve the idea.

The group agrees that this strategy will prod the boss to offer constructive criticism. Above all, it will show him the value of teamwork.

Delphi Method

The *Delphi* technique is another popular way of using a group of people to brainstorm solutions. Originally, the Delphi method was developed at the Rand Corporation (in Santa Monica, California) as a method for long-range forecasting. Today, it is widely adopted by problem solvers in industry, in the military, and in applied research. The beauty of the technique is that it distills the thinking of many people, without requiring them ever to meet.

HOW TO USE THE DELPHI METHOD

1. *Query the participants about how to solve a problem.* For example, they might be asked: "In what way might this product be changed to make it more convenient to use, without worrying at this point about specific cost restrictions?" The group then ponders this question for a few days before sending in responses.

2. *Distribute a summary of the answers to all participants.* Nobody is told who made which statement.

3. *Ask the group for additional suggestions, along with evaluations of the other participants' suggestions.*

4. *Distribute the new answers together with the comments.* At this point, the participants have a clear idea of the thinking of the other members. The leader of the group is responsible for summarizing these responses. After this airing of the different viewpoints, the participants are again permitted to revise their answers, and are asked for comments.

5. *During the final step, the participants receive a review of the comments, together with the answers to the questions.* The participants are again invited to alter their answers.

6. *After the long cross-fertilization, what should emerge is a consensus of opinion as well as a wide span of viewpoints.* Obviously, this is not a method for handling emergencies or for seeking a quick and simple solution. However, it is a valuable way to get a cross section of viewpoints.

Attribute Listing and the Osborn Checklist

An analytical spur to creativity is *attribute listing*, particularly when used in combination with a checklist developed by the late advertising pioneer Alex Osborn. Osborn, one of the founders of the New York advertising firm of Batten, Barten, Durstine and Osborn, urged account executives to use his checklist to find ways to improve a product.

HOW TO USE ATTRIBUTE LISTING AND THE OSBORN CHECKLIST

1. *List all the attributes of a product or procedure.* If, for example, you want to develop better use of your office space,

begin by listing the principal attributes of that space and the functions performed there. List the number of workers, their functions, their system of supervision, their schedules, etc.

2. *Evaluate each of these attributes in terms of the questions on the following checklist:*

- How can I put it to other uses?
- How can I adapt it?
- How can I modify it?
- How can I magnify it?
- How can I minify it?
- How can I substitute it?
- How can I rearrange it?

WARNING: When you are stumped by one aspect of a problem, don't give up. Just go on to the next step, and try to solve that. If you find answers for the rest of the problem, the solution to the unknown piece may become obvious. General Douglas MacArthur profited from this stepping-stone approach. During his victorious island hopping, MacArthur was sometimes forced to bypass an island before moving on to his next triumph. The ones he couldn't conquer eventually surrendered after being cut off from the captured islands.

10. STUDY THE RISKS

Problem: So Many Risks!

"I think we should continue reaching the suburban audiences by offering them cultural entertainment with subscription seats," declared Edith Moore to her partner, John Anderson. Managing directors of a Philadelphia theater, they were considering their target audience for the upcoming season. "I feel we should go with a program of popular entertainers—black soul and some white mainstream people—to get a larger share of the local audience. We may not net as much profit, because of the price of booking such performers, but at least we reach a wider community audience," John said.

"I agree we should move away from our elitist image," Edith said. "But we also have a third choice: use the theater for national touring companies. It might be a little riskier financially than the program of subscription tickets for local opera and ballet companies. But it would certainly give us more of a national reputation," she concluded.

"So what do we do?" John asked. "There are so many risks. We sure could use a crystal ball now."

*　　*　　*　　*　　*

Step 10: Study the Risks

Decision making, as Auren Uris notes, "involves a certain amount of risk," since many future uncertainties may threaten any course of action you choose. One doesn't need a crystal ball, however, to anticipate the consequences of a decision. Of course, it is impossible to second-guess all the possible risks, but a systematic study of the alternatives in complicated decisions can help you know what to expect.

If you have used the building-block approach outlined so far, you already have an inside track on understanding the problem and on knowing what you want to accomplish with the solution.

At this point, you should start narrowing your choices by seeing where they might take you. You might find that an alternative that looks promising in theory is too risky in practice. You can begin narrowing the choices as you examine the potential risks.

How to Study the Risks

1. *List the alternative solutions on paper.*

2. *Imagine the decision in operation and list the problems that could arise.* Some factors to consider: Are your timetables realistic? Will this strain your manpower, material, facilities, etc.? Ask yourself repeatedly, "How serious is it if the 'worst' does happen, and how likely is that probability?"

3. *Evaluate the likelihood that each of these problems will occur.* Kepner and Tregoe suggest that you rate these along a scale of 1 to 10. The most probable would receive a 10, and would become the standard by which to evaluate the likelihood of the other problems. Arnold, in *The Art of Decision Making*, proposes another scale: high, medium, or low.

4. *Rate the possible impact of each problem.* Use the rating system that you chose in #3 above. In addition, you might find

it helpful to describe briefly, in a phrase, the possible impacts. Consider how each problem might affect your decision.

5. *Examine your risk assessment of each solution.* It is at this point that you might decide to eliminate or modify an alternative that poses too great a risk.

WARNING: To make a sound decision, it is not always necessary to have all the facts; however, to evaluate the risk in a decision, it is important to know what information is lacking. When you are not absolutely clear about how your decision will work, it is better to allow a margin of safety for the unexpected.

11. EVALUATE
THE ALTERNATIVES

Problem: Which One to Go With?

"I like all three ideas, but I'm really going to have to make a decision soon about which one to go with," Geoffrey Wagner thought to himself. Wagner, vice-president of a major department store, had solicited ideas from his staff on how the store could attract more customers and improve its image in order to meet the competition created by a new department store across the street. His call for ideas had brought forth a paper blizzard, and he now found himself favoring three possible solutions: a new advertising campaign, a new and streamlined design for the store's interior, and the creation of a stylish restaurant and bar in the basement.

"All three proposals would bring in more customers," Wagner thought to himself, "but how am I going to pick the best one?"

* * * * *

Step 11: Evaluate the Alternatives

You have come to the point where you must select from the alternatives to find the one that most effectively fulfills the needs of the decision. Decision making requires experience, knowledge, common sense, and judgment, but careful analysis is the most important ingredient. By intelligently evaluating your choices, weighing them against your criteria, and anticipating their risks and consequences, you should arrive at the best solution. You have already studied the possible risks of your alternatives; now evaluate how your alternatives measure up in crucial areas.

How to Evaluate Alternatives

1. *Analyze which alternative offers the greatest economy of effort.* As Drucker suggests, you must look carefully at which of the possible lines of action will give the greatest results with the least effort. An ideal solution will solve the problem with a minimum of expense and disruption.

2. *Reexamine the degree of change required and the schedule you want to adopt.* If you believe the situation has great urgency, you might lean toward a dramatic solution that would involve an all-out effort to solve the problem. On the other hand, you might opt for a quieter approach when you want gradually and unobtrusively to integrate a change into the everyday routine.

3. *Examine closely what Uris calls the "resources factor."* Which solution best takes advantage of the resources at your disposal? You might feel that alternative A has more advantages than alternative B but decide to go with alternative B since it involves a piece of equipment that is easily available. Or you might find a subordinate of such outstanding skill that alternative B becomes more desirable because this employee is available to carry it out.

4. *Consider the delegation and supervision realities in your organization.* Perhaps your organization structure poses prob-

lems in implementing one of the alternatives. Or maybe you believe that your employees are not ready for the change in procedures involved in one of the alternatives.

5. *Measure each alternative against the criteria checklist* (see p. 42). Begin by noting that any alternative under serious consideration should automatically satisfy an absolute requirement. If not, discard it. It is important that you weed these alternatives out at the beginning so that you can narrow the field down to the serious candidates.

Now rate the alternatives against each of the remaining desirable objectives on your criteria checklist. Using a 10-high scale, rate each alternative the same way you rated each criterion. This approach is adapted from methods suggested by Kepner and Tregoe, Arnold, and Emery, among others. How does this alternative measure up in the requirements of the criterion? If no alternative does a perfect job of satisfying a particular criterion, the one that comes closest rates a 10. In turn, the alternative that fails completely to fulfill a criterion will get the lowest ranking next to that criterion.

Multiply the rating of the criterion by the rating of the alternative, and then measure how the alternatives compare. Let's say you give ratings of 5 to the way that one alternative meets the requirements of a criterion rated 7; the result is 35. Go through each alternative and multiply the ranking of that alternative next to the value of the criterion. Then add up the scores for each alternative (an example is given on p. 59). Pay particular attention to how an alternative fulfills a top-ranking criterion. After assessing the results, you may decide to go with the alternative that scores highest in terms of the top-ranking criterion. Or you might decide to go with the one that scores highest all around.

The Factor Review Task Force should work with you to assess these alternatives; you might give them the job of measuring the alternatives against the criteria, and then meet with them to discuss their findings.

6. *Don't underestimate the value of your hunches.* Sometimes you may have only your intuition or your gut feeling when

Matching Your Alternatives Against the Criteria

Below is an example of how you can use your checklist of criteria to assess each of the alternatives suggested to Geoffrey Wagner at the beginning of this chapter. To the left of each criteria is your priority for it. Underneath each alternative is the rating that reflects how that alternative measures up next to the criterion. At the bottom is the sum total of how each alternative shapes up against all the desirable objectives.

Priority	Desirable objectives	A new ad campaign	Restaurant and bar	Redecorate the interior
10	Appeal to young buyers	× 8 = 80	× 9 = 90	× 9 = 90
10	Appeal to budget-conscious buyers	× 10 = 100	× 3 = 30	× 0 = 0
10	Give wider visibility to the store in outlying suburbs	× 10 = 100	× 5 = 50	× 0 = 0
9	Modernize image	× 9 = 81	× 10 = 90	× 10 = 90
7	Expand range of services	× 0 = 0	× 8 = 56	× 0 = 0
	TOTALS	361	316	180

deciding between two solutions that seem equally attractive. Effective decision makers know that intuition backed by judgment, intelligence, and experience is an invaluable built-in decision-making tool.

7. *Look critically at your top choice.* Emery warns managers against selling themselves and others on an alternative that *seems* attractive. He advises them at this stage to try their best to shoot down the frontrunner. Using your earlier study of risks (see p. 54), consider what could go wrong with this choice, and what the odds are that this problem will occur. Are contingency plans available? Make this analysis before adopting your final choice.

8. *Choose the best alternative after discussing the matter with your staff and/or Factor Review Task Force.* Does everybody agree that this is the right choice? What are the objections? Be sure to ask yourself these questions suggested by Sanderson in *Successful Problem Management*: Am I being realistic about the strengths and weaknesses of this decision? Is my decision adaptable to change? Have I planned as far as it is possible to plan? And finally, do I have a reserve plan to fall back on in case of an emergency?

Always have alternative solutions on hand, so you can shift gears if things don't work out as planned. As Drucker notes, "A decision without an alternative is a desperate gambler's throw."

WARNING: Don't be afraid of merging solutions. Never overlook the possibility of combining solutions when you have reached this stage of the analysis and believe that no one alternative fits the bill. The best solution often combines elements from two or more of your alternatives.

---

12. TEST THE DECISION

Problem: Will It Float?

"I'm beginning to have second thoughts about the idea," Julie Simmons, vice-president at Image advertising agency, remarked to Steven Nederlander, one of the firm's account executives. The two were debating the merits of initiating a flex-time schedule among the creative staff—copywriters and art staff. After months of lobbying for a different work schedule, the creative staff had persuaded management to give them a staggered workweek. But now Simmons was reconsidering.

"On the face of it, it certainly seems reasonable enough," Nederlander said. "But I guess you're worried about how our clients will feel about it. I wish there was some way to try out the new schedule, and see if it floats."

*   *   *   *   *

Step 12: Test the Decision

There is a way out of the dilemma. The agency can test the new idea—give it a trial run. It is a mistake to believe that once a decision is made, it is written in stone—irreversible and final. And putting your decision on an experimental basis is often the best way to validate it.

No matter now exhaustively you have analyzed the situation and studied its possible consequences, there is always the potential for problems. First, there is the problem of whether the new system works. Second, there may be a safety question. If new technology is used, you might want to test the system for hidden dangers. Or you may want to check that enough safeguards have been incorporated. Finally, it is difficult to know in advance how the new system will operate. Have you allocated enough personnel to the new system? Is the schedule realistic? The answer: test your decision.

How to Test the Decision

1. *Give the decision a trial run.* In many cases, it is possible to try out a decision short of full implementation. This trial run will let you see how your decision works, and allow you to make changes at an early and flexible stage.

2. *Develop a decision with "branching steps."* This technique, suggested by Auren Uris among others, calls for a limited implementation of the decision. This approach allows you to compare the results with those produced by an alternative solution or by existing conditions. For example, half the creative staff at Image could have gone on a flex-time schedule while the remainder stayed on their present schedule, and management could have compared the results.

3. *Make changes when problems arise.* Be flexible. This is the most opportune time to improve or change your decision—before it becomes fully operational. It may simply be a matter of changing personnel or of replacing a faulty part.

PART 3: Making the decision work

Make sure that everything is ready. Establish a feedback mechanism so you can follow your solution in its transition from the drawing board to the real world.

13. SELL YOUR DECISION

Problem: Convincing Others

"I'm afraid I'll never be able to convince Dorothy Phelps about the value of the plan," Sylvia Zwerling complained to one of her colleagues. "Dorothy has told me—and more than once—that she thinks the whole idea of lawyers advertising is unprofessional and crass." Zwerling, a partner in a women's law firm, had decided that the best way to let the community know about their new firm was to advertise in the local paper. Unfortunately, she now realized she might encounter resistance from one of the older and more traditional members of the firm.

"I'm afraid it might be better just to forget the whole idea," Sylvia noted with discouragement. "I can't imagine changing Dorothy's mind."

* * * * *

Step 13: Sell Your Decision

Sylvia Zwerling is giving up too easily: a skillful presentation of her arguments might have overcome Dorothy's opposition.

Presenting your decision to top management for approval can be one of the hardest parts of the decision-making process. At this stage, however, you have several important points in your favor: you have thoroughly researched, studied, and evaluated the problem and the alternative solutions; and you probably have the cooperation of your associates, since you have been working with them from the start. Now you will have to show those above you in the hierarchy why you have come to your decision. And, if your subordinates have not played a major role in reaching the decision, you may also need to explain your choice to them and motivate them to carry it out. As this book has already pointed out, the trend in management theory today is to involve employees all the way down the line in the decisions.

How to Sell Your Decision

1. *State exactly what will be accomplished, and how.* You will make a stronger case by presenting your conclusions first, i.e., what the decision will achieve, Fred DeArmond points out in *The Executive at Work*. Then develop your case with evidence, precedents, views of outside authorities, and other relevant background material and analysis. Be as brief as possible, since you don't want to waste the time either of your superiors or your subordinates.

2. *Have all the facts at your fingertips.* It is not good enough, for example, to say that you hope to increase productivity with your plan, or that it will help the company reach a larger share of the market. Have the figures handy to show what your plan will achieve, and how. Justify the expenditures in terms of the estimated returns, both in the short- and long-term.

3. *Be ready to counter objections.* Since your evaluation of alternatives should have exposed most of the shortcomings that might be used by the opposition, be able to show how you will avoid the most serious problems. Check to see whether your

ideas have already been tried. If they have failed, find out why. What steps will you take to avoid the same mistakes?

Rehearse your presentation with an associate who can play the adversary role. The rehearsal will give you confidence for the actual presentation.

4. *Be optimistic and positive when presenting your ideas.* Show your own commitment to the plan, and try to communicate your enthusiasm to others. A decision expressed with resolution and confidence, Uris states in *The Executive Deskbook*, has a much higher likelihood of success.

5. *Try to convince people that it is to their advantage to carry out the decision.* Tell them—and show them, if possible—*how* it will make things better for them as well as for the organization.

WARNING: Be flexible and listen to the comments and criticism of others. Don't summarily reject a suggestion from one of your workers just because you have decided that your decision is the best of all possible solutions. Somebody involved closely in the daily routine might have spotted something you missed.

---

14. GET EVERYTHING READY

Problem: How Could I Forget?

"What an embarrassment! I could have kicked myself for forgetting such a simple thing," Harry Wheatley said to a colleague, Alice Brown, as they sat in Harry's office. "I had arranged everything for the inventory, days ahead of time. I had hired three temps to help out, arranged extra office space, and rented special machines to analyze the results," Harry recalled, shaking his head.

"And what happened?" Alice asked.

"Well, I realized on the first day of the inventory that I had forgotten something important. You know those special check-off forms I ordered? Well, they required a special pencil so the machines could read them . . . So, of course, I forgot to order the pencils and didn't tell anyone else to do it either!"

*   *   *   *   *

Step 14: Get Everything Ready

Everything must be prepared before you start to implement your decision. You must make sure that all the material, facilities, and manpower are ready and available—or will be when you need them. At the same time, you must delegate responsibility and authority to those who will carry out the decision.

Resources

You or members of your staff should draw up a checklist of everything that is needed, and when. Make sure that these resources will be available according to schedule. Refer back to the research that was conducted when you began the hunt for alternatives (see p. 44).

Go through the decision step by step to make sure you have accounted for all the necessary resources. You or a subordinate must get the people and resources organized and ready. It may seem unnecessary to emphasize this point, but, as Uris notes, many a decision, made after days or weeks of effort, fails to produce results simply because "the decision is followed up in such a weak fashion." And getting everything planned and ready is crucial to making sure that the decision does work.

HOW TO ORGANIZE YOUR RESOURCES

1. *Check whether all the personnel are ready for the job.* Have they familiarized themselves with the new routine, technology, etc.? Are they aware of their deadlines? Do they have all the skills for the job? If you run short of workers for the project, do you know where to get more? As K.F. Jackson notes in *The Art of Solving Problems*, everything that we design to solve a problem

will have to be suited in some manner "to the needs and abilities of the people who are going to have to work with the product."
2. *Make sure all the necessary material is on hand or easily available*. Is the quantity adequate? Are your quality standards met? The consensus among management experts is that a checklist will help you keep track here. While drawing up the list of your material resources, ask yourself the following or related questions: Have you made all the necessary provisions for handling and storage? Have you or your staff checked to see that the material is in satisfactory condition? Do you know where to go if you run short? Have you made sure that the safety precautions are adequate?
3. *Ascertain that you have access to the right facilities*. Are there enough machines for the job? Will you have to rent or buy more? Is the space adequate? Have you made all the transportation arrangements? Will these facilities be available for as long as you need them? Do you have the authorization to use these facilities for as long as necessary? Have you or a subordinate checked these facilities recently to make sure that everything is in working order?

Delegation

Delegation of responsibility and authority is vital for carrying out the decision successfully. Select the individuals carefully and prepare them thoroughly for the responsibilities. Decisions should be delegated to the lowest level where they can be made intelligently by employees possessing the relevant facts and required judgment.

HOW TO DELEGATE

1. *Give careful consideration to assigning the right person to the right responsibilities*. Jackson suggests that you first determine what qualities the supervisor needs, and then match the person to the job. Also, ask yourself what qualities the person should *not* have. You might decide, for instance, that you do not want a

supervisor who is not thoroughly familiar with the plant operation—which would, of course, eliminate newly hired employees.

2. *Institute a feedback mechanism to supply you with timely reports.* A signaling system is suggested in the next chapter (see p. 74). Encourage communication between supervisors and workers, so that problems are immediately reported and can be swiftly acted upon.

3. *Spell out in writing what you want accomplished.* Jackson suggests you develop a chart that shows what you want to happen, where, and when. Your staff will then be able to see exactly what role their department should play, and how their role fits into the larger picture. As an alternative, you might simply list the duties to be performed. Above all, it's important that all employees in a coordinated project know exactly what their jobs and responsibilities are.

4. *Be sure that you and your subordinates have the authority to carry out every step of the plan.* It is not enough to know that you have access to certain facilities; make sure that you have the authority to use those facilities when you need them.

5. *Give those delegated to supervise the decision the power to act effectively.* It is important that your supervisors "speak in your name," DeArmond says in *The Executive at Work*, "expecting that you will back them up in every reasonable way." This kind of authority is particularly important if an emergency arises, since the supervisor must act immediately and independently.

6. *Delegate authority following the lines of authority in your organization.* Delegating authority over somebody's head or setting up a system of command that runs counter to the procedures of your organization can create serious problems.

WARNING: Don't rely too heavily on one person—or one small group—to carry out the decision. Overburdening employees with expectations might well end up in failure of the project. If you distribute responsibilities fairly and intelligently, one person or one group is unlikely to emerge as the weak link that dooms a decision.

15. FOLLOW THROUGH

Problem: In Other Hands

"There are a hundred and one details to be covered," Alice Patterson thought to herself as she surveyed the stack of manuscripts and memos piled on top of the managing editor's desk. "I wish I were better at following through," she reflected as she made her way back to her office. Director of new publications at Worldwide Communications, Alice had spent the last year developing a new magazine for young mothers and was now at the critical juncture where her brainchild was about to leave the preliminary editorial stage.

"I shouldn't worry. The project is in good hands. Shirley is a talented managing editor, and Ray is one of the best art directors around," she consoled herself, only to lapse again into doubts. "I really feel I should take a more direct role. But honestly, I don't know where to begin."

*   *   *   *   *

Step 15: Follow Through on the Decision

A new project must be carefully shepherded through its early and most vulnerable stages. Alice Patterson, for example, should take a more direct role in her project as it leaves the drawing board. She needs to set up a timetable and a monitoring system to alert her to exactly where and when to intervene. Good planning and an attention to details and priorities are the main consideration—and they can be learned.

In addition, she should be on the lookout for ways to improve the project.

How to Establish a Monitoring System

1. *Establish your priorities.* Make sure that the most important elements of your plan or decision receive the most attention. In the case mentioned above, Alice Patterson should decide which areas to involve herself in. For instance, she might want to study carefully the cover design and copy, since this is what immediately draws people to a publication. In this area, she should retain direct supervision and final approval.

2. *Translate broad goals into measurable activities.* For example, if you are devising a new production schedule, tell your employees exactly what they have to do to meet projected increases in production. It is not enough to say that you expect your sales staff to work hard in selling a new product; work with them on a marketing strategy and specify what quotas you expect them to fill.

3. *Create a timetable.* Make sure that those involved know the schedule. The schedule must have checkpoints to allow you to follow the progress of the new procedure or innovation. Returning to the case above, Alice might tell her editors and art staff that she wants final approval of the artwork and layout before it goes to the printer, and give them a deadline when the artwork must be ready for her viewing.

4. *Be realistic about schedules.* Allow a margin of time for

workers to familiarize themselves with a new procedure or technology. It is also important to have this safety margin for contingencies that might arise when something new or unfamiliar is introduced into the daily operation.

5. *Use "clockwise" or "counterclockwise" planning to develop a timetable.* These methods, proposed by Emery in *The Compleat Manager*, break down the decision into separate components to allow you to plan and monitor the different stages. They allow you to see how all the essential pieces fit together within a time framework. In clockwise planning, you begin by identifying the *first* step of the plan, estimate how long it will take, and then judge the time required for each successive step. Focus on the results that you expect at the end of each stage of the decision. Have you made realistic estimates of the time and money allocated to each stage?

On the other hand, counterclockwise planning works backward from completion date to the present. Working backward, the manager decides exactly what should be accomplished during each stage of implementation.

6. *Be sure contingency and backup plans are prepared.* Have you carefully worked out the contingency plans with those delegated to carry out the decision? Are replacements in personnel and material available in case of an emergency?

7. *Set up controls and reporting procedures.* These will enable you to follow the progress of the decision. Decide how you want the reports to be made—by phone, memo, whatever—but be sure they are presented to you periodically.

How can you follow up on your decision, particularly if you are far removed from its day-to-day operation? Oxenfeldt, Miller, and Dickinson, in *A Basic Approach to Executive Decision Making*, suggest that a signaling system will help you monitor the progress of your decision and will function as an Early Warning System to identify problems.

- *Develop a model—a standard of operations and productivity—that will be your yardstick for measuring the progress of the decision.* These figures may be in the form of production quotas, sales figures, etc. The

point is to have performance figures that will help
you gauge the success or failure of the decision.
- *Set a target level for performance standards.* This target
will help you—and the employees working to meet
the standards—see whether everything is working
according to plan. At the same time, identify a
threshold point: if performance falls below that point,
you know something is wrong.
- *Develop a procedure that will supply you with regular reports
on this signaling system.* The reports will inform you
whether target levels are being met, and alert you
immediately if performance has dipped below the
threshold point. Reporting can be in the form of
memos or a phone call. The point, as Oxenfeldt,
Miller, and Dickinson stress, is to provide the manager with a concise and convenient monitoring system, with a minimum of paperwork.

How to Improve the Decision

Even if your monitoring and signaling systems have
shown no hidden problems, don't rest on your laurels. Every
decision can be improved; perhaps a better strategy can be
devised the next time around. Always be on the alert to make
adjustments and changes.

1. *Keep a log of the changes, modifications, problems, repairs,
or adjustments that you make during the early stages in the decision's
implementation.* According to Jackson, this record will provide
you with useful information for preventive maintenance and
future improvements.

2. *Ask yourself if the solution can be improved—even if it was a
success.* Sanderson suggests that question in *Successful Problem
Management.* Perhaps the personnel change worked better than
anticipated, and now you can start to think about giving the
new employee more responsibilities. Perhaps you were modest

in your initial expectations and now feel you can raise your standards.

3. *Identify both the strong and weak points of the solution.* Once you have recognized these critical points, you may be able to bolster the strengths and minimize the weaknesses. Ask yourself what you have learned from this experience, and how you can apply it to other situations. Will you be better equipped to handle a similar situation in the future?

4. *Ask yourself what the unforeseen problems were and why they arose.* It is impossible to anticipate every problem or loophole, but it is important to see where you were misled in your thinking. Now that the pressure is off, you can begin to tighten the new procedures or tinker with your planning.

WARNING: Questions to keep in mind: Have you prepared for outside forces or unexpected contingencies? Could they unexpectedly and adversely affect what you have done? Will changes in the economy, new policies in the company, or personnel changes disrupt the system? Have you made your decision flexible enough to handle those changes?

CONCLUSION

Decision making, as Peter F. Drucker notes, "can no longer be improvised." It is becoming less and less feasible to rely on intuitive inspiration in a complex and sophisticated business world, where everyday decisions may pose complex risks and far-reaching economic consequences. Decisions based on instinct rather than knowledge and analysis, aimed at adapting to rather than transcending the problem, could prove jerry-built in this business environment.

Systematic decision making can be laborious, particularly if you are dealing with complicated problems. The temptation in these cases is to take shortcuts, to develop on the wing a solution that might successfully meet your requirements. The hard work of careful analysis, however, will pay off—in more ways than just in fulfilling your immediate goal. The knowledge gained from your research will help you deal with other related problems, provide you with a clearer idea of the resources and capabilities of your operation, and give you much-needed experience in decision making. It will also instill confidence in your thinking among your staff, your co-workers, and your superiors.

And once you have thought through alternatives, you have something to fall back on if your chosen alternative proves a failure.

At the same time, you have used both your imagination and your analytical mind to arrive at your final destination. And this may be the last point that should be made—that creativity and logic are not mutually exclusive but are rather the basis of resourceful management. Following the techniques used in this book should allow you to intelligently use both these touchstones of effective problem solving and decision making.

Bibliography

Ackoff, Russell L. *The Art of Problem Solving.* New York: John Wiley & Sons, 1978.

Arnold, John D. *The Art of Decision Making.* New York: AMACOM Paperback, 1978.

DeArmond, Fred. *The Executive at Work.* Englewood Cliffs, N.J.: Prentice-Hall, 1958.

Drucker, Peter F. *The Effective Executive.* New York: Harper & Row, 1967.

———. *The Practice of Management.* New York: Harper & Row, 1954.

Emery, David A. *The Compleat Manager.* New York: McGraw-Hill, 1970.

Jackson, K. F. *The Art of Solving Problems.* New York: St. Martin's, 1975.

Kepner, Charles H. and Tregoe, Benjamin B. *The Rational Manager: A Systematic Approach to Problem Solving and Decision Making.* New York: McGraw-Hill, 1965.

Oxenfeldt, Alfred R.; Miller, David W.; and Dickinson, Roger A. *A Basic Approach to Executive Decision Making.* New York: AMACOM, 1964.

Reynolds, Helen and Tramel, Mary E. *Executive Time Management.* Englewood Cliffs, N.J.: Prentice-Hall, 1979.

Prince, George M. *The Practice of Creativity.* New York: Collier Books, 1970.

Sanderson, Michael. *Personal Guide to Identifying and Solving Problems Quickly.* New York: Executive Enterprises Publications Co., Inc., 1981.

———. *Successful Problem Management.* New York: Wiley-Interscience, 1976.

———. *What's the Problem Here? Time-Saving Problem-Solving Techniques for the Manager.* New York: Mercury Press (a division of Executive Enterprises Publications Co., Inc.), 1981.

Uris, Auren. *The Executive Deskbook,* 2nd ed. New York: Van Nostrand Reinhold Co., 1976.